Apterous
Dreams
And
Birds

Apterous Dreams And Birds

WESLEY FRANZ

◯◯◯ MAIDA VALE PUBLISHING

First published in 2018
by Maida Vale Publishing Ltd
Suite 333, 19-21 Crawford Street
Marylebone, London W1H 1PJ
United Kingdom

Cover design and typeset by Edwin Smet
Printed in England by TJ International Ltd, Padstow, Cornwall

ISBN 978-1-912477-60-9

WWW.EYEWEARPUBLISHING.COM

This is dedicated to
Edith Jean Kimney Aldoor,
a wonderful and hortatory teacher.

Wesley Franz
has lived in São Paulo for many
years where he studied and graduated as an engineer.
He worked in industry for twenty-nine years. Recently,
he has been teaching and giving support in English for
his students, most of them physicians and PhD students
in fields relating to biology. His poetic influences include
W. Carlos Williams, Ted Hughes, Philip Larkin, Keats,
J. Cabral, C.D. Andrade and F. Pessoa, to name a few.
In 1969, as a teenager, he participated in a poetry contest
where he satirized the military of that time. These
shenanigans brought censorship and threats, and he
was told never to write verse again. Some years later
he started – and still is – disobeying. He loves regular
feijoada, and spends time chatting with friends
and sailing. Married, with a son and a daughter,
he writes whenever 'inspiration'
strikes – usually.

TABLE OF CONTENTS

THE MINERAL SONG

When one chases the Mineral Song
music can be found,
consisting of structures
non-musical to our human ears.

Step by step, a percussion,
eventually a rhythm, a pace,
this is when the Mineral Song
shows its lovely violent grace;
in a volcanic eruption,
when an earthquake shows its face.

Mighty boulder silence
can also be a tempo
within the structure-material
of the Mineral Song.

The Earth-old Mineral Song;
understand its stone-words,
structure (human or not),
enjoy it.

SCARY SCARECROWS

The idea is to feel effectively space-time,
to play with the happiness
of only partially-understood chaos,
and find the butterfly effect almost everywhere;

to have a high with the Principle of Uncertainty,
fall in love with superstrings
whilst observing a solemn buzzard,
and re-write the Seventh Law of Thermodynamics

The idea is to scatter scary scarecrows
all over the reason-ideas space;
maybe they'll get really scared,
lose that monotonous rectilinear rectitude
transforming into delicious curves.

SMOOTH SHADOWS IN THE NIGHT

How can there be shadows in the night?
A real night's really dark,
how can there be shadows with no light?

But there are, with absolutely no light.
They are shadows of the night.
It doesn't mean they are visible.
What can one see with no light?
But then exist they do,
oblivious of me and you.

Many things, structures,
perhaps exist if we decide so.
Some images, solid superstrings,
one can only conceive.

Dark night with playful shadows,
our childish, pure concepts
of the soft shadows in the night.

LIFE IN A BIG CITY

They insist on moving
inside their cars and bodies
maybe riding two-wheeled machines,
crowding streets and so-called avenues,
moving back and forth
like coordinated ants in their colony.

They convey intrinsic messages
fostered by their sexual organs and stomachs
(precisely in that order)
inspired by nothing but their own truths;
some truths, some messages.

They fall, but do not perish
inspired by the internal organs
to gather money; hopes and frustrations,
resembling lost soldiers in a battle,
pure biological fanfare.

CABRAL'S VULTURE REVISTED

In the dry desert, this noble vulture
readies his beak and claws,
preparing for his civil servant services,
regular duties of a serious Professional.

All grey and black,
wearing that serious look
with avuncular manners, umbrella wings,
treating with effective euthanasia
the not-so-dead, man or beast;
complete cleaning services
delivered on finishing the feast.

Maybe working, yes, at a lower rank
but offering indispensable action –
such a proficient Professional.

IMPRESSIONS FROM SUNRISES

There are many kinds of sunrises:
watch them daily
out in the open; if not,
inside your lonely room.

The sun appearing,
glue your glance to the ceiling,
listen to the paragraphs of your thoughts.

ORDINARY DAY

An absolutely ordinary day,
lackadaisical sunrise
conveying unpretentious light.

People think regularly then
about their regular chores.

He doesn't think at all, he feels
under his feet the regular rotation
of this Earth around that Sun.

THE ACROBATIC ASTRONAUT
– PART I

I Observations from the Space Station

An Astronaut-Observer is remembering
his views and images of those earthly things
some dare call nice, charming, classic and inspiring,
like an afternoon breeze gently blowing
across a field of gardenias.

Our Astronaut-Dreamer remembers
those strange events, like movie-going,
with lots of eyes watching but not seeing.
He remembers those happy lights
puncturing the night of a city.
Seen there, they glitter and shine;
seen from here, they twinkle, and fade
like inverted stars.

II Beyond Loneliness

Our Astronaut-Worker is saddened
because he misses something
he is trying to define, but then
he feels complete with solid emptiness.

He decides to observe and study again
the blue planet beneath, now so distant
it says nothing new to him.

Then he turns to his new surroundings,
writing verse about the metal and plastic
structures around him; he takes pains
to sing about the panels, alloys and hoses,
gauges and switches.

Weightless, floating inside the station,
he gazes at the blue planet Earth,
again finding needed inspiration
and describes then what it's worth.

Scattered on the surface and a little above,
he sees men moving, going, doing
the strange, odd things that also sent him here
trying still to reach his own goals.

III *The Astronaut's Conclusion*

He arrives at the gist: Man-Astronaut
must find Poetry and sense Inspiration
wherever it is: in gardenia fields, hills,
the wind, metal, sights, genes or spaceships.

The music, the verse shall forever
be completely intrinsic and *fiercely attached*
to our Human-Astronaut-Observer.

TIME AND KALASHNIKOVS

From your first car-crash
you came out unbruised and alive
after that 100 + mph episode,
your time-mind no longer virginal.

Over the next days,
the colours got brighter,
scents stronger and more fluid,
providing the feeling of being reborn.

You got older and your time-frames
changed, as if with yourself
the mind was playing games.
Ten years ago seemed
just some two years past.

Then again you survived
when colourless assassins
were kalashnikoving the crowd,
spraying metallic injustice,
sparing no children there.

Again you experienced
those renewed tastes, colours and scents.

Bombs exploded in trains,
tragic loss of lives,
scattered human remains.

Insistently alive, stained with blood,
you found a gold-ringed finger,
a handless finger, a lady's
because of the nail well-done.
You couldn't tell if it was wedding
or engagement because you couldn't say
from which hand it was thrown away.

So again a survivor.
Times come over and upon you,
your own time, our time.

How can we be oblivious?

How can we be oblivious?

TOO MUCH NEWS

On the radio, in the newspaper,
on the machine once called TV,
talking with other human beings,
eavesdropping in a bar
on a lovely lonely evening –
too much news.

Some people are hungry,
others over-fed.
We should do something.
Most of us do nothing,
but we're not guilty really,
afterall, it's in the News;
someone responsible should do something,
you see, it *is* in the News.

News, facts and suppositions.
X was all the rage last summer,
yeah, it made the headlines.

Comprehensive, daily coverage
of what's going on,

regardless of what really matters
makes one feel wise, smart
and the power of Information
makes you feel a better man.

Then one day, the power went down:
no TV, no Radio, no machine.
An electric tempest silenced all radiowaves.
The mailman didn't come,
the phone didn't ring.

That day, serendipitously,
we were nicely bloated with oblivion;
but then, honestly so.

TELEVISION TODAY

It is turned on, capturing our attention
as usual, with the normal downpour
of information which can build an idea
about something, and also
modify impressions, if we are to imagine
subtly, that quiet lack of imagination
belonging to the deep basements
of our empty souls.

Some souls, some emptiness.

MENTAL PILLOWS

He is floating
through this reckless life
of wine and cigarettes.

'Tomorrow' is
a comfortable question;
questions have been
the pillows of his sleep.

Questions, questions.
A lack of answers makes them
whole, heavy and powerful
and very, very comfortable.

SCHRÖDINGER'S CAT
REVISITED

If I don't look
you aren't there,
if I don't care
you won't move.

But if I look
there you are,
and if I watch
something must be.

Then I look
but I don't see,
and if I see
what will it be?

Can I comfortably dare
absolutely not to care?
Should we quietly stay
waiting for that glorious
other day?

May we toast it all with oblivion?

What can be said with precision?

TOMORROW MORNING

Tomorrow morning,
I will wake up
if I survive my dreams.

Tomorrow morning,
I shall have some tea
if I can manage the kettle.

Tomorrow morning,
I will take a shower
if I find the bathroom.

If, tomorrow morning,
I don't see you around the house
I shall do some thinking.

Tomorrow morning,
I must remember that
tomorrow will only be
tomorrow.

APTEROUS DREAMS

This young crowd can be found
in the cities of richer countries.
They have a very peculiar trait
of being half-masters of their fate,
hanging on apterous dreams.

Another young crowd
dwelling in the slums of the world,
all their dreams depend on addiction,
addiction to something subtle
which some call Hope.

THE ACROBATIC ASTRONAUT
– PART II

We should check again the activities of our
       friend
the Acrobatic Astronaut, there above us,
floating in the space station, floating in space,
again observing ordinary so-so earthly life.

Getting bored of watching some reckless,
bland and sometimes just plainly stupid
things that men on earth insist on doing,
he suddenly gets gravely concerned
about his surroundings, and his mind,
not entirely programmed, just an ordinary
human mind, starts to work, to design,
       to imagine.

There, alone, he talks to the people on Earth:

"Hey, hello, how's that, yeah, it's lonely
       out here.
I have only one clear idea of what to do."

He will send a message in a bottle,
like a professional castaway.

Message from A.A.

'I am an astronaut at the space station,
drifting, captured by gravitational currents.
I must tell the ones that will come after me,
the many who will come after me:

Please find and stalk Inspiration
on these instruments, hoses, bolts
panels, devices, circuits, software
because even with all those now Atomic
nano-controls here in the space station
or on Earth there beneath, I gingerly state:

Still you shall be human and therefore frail,
Poetic Inspiration to be your holy grail.'

So now, happy and relieved
our Acrobatic Astronaut returns
to his regular, so scientific chores.

The farce continuing on Earth
he consciously ignores.

WINDOWS

Windows are found everywhere:
windows in your car, windows in your house,
windows in that oh-so comfortable hotel,
windows in a picture, a photography of windows.

Some can be opened, then shut.
You can just manage to open
and then shut, and open them again;
you are playing with windows.

Men build walls but walls isolate.
We are not meant to be separate,
so clearly we need windows.

Telescopes floating above our atmosphere
provide us with a very special sort of window,
from where we can do some eavesdropping
into this astonishing universe.

TALL BUILDINGS

I place a glass on top of the fridge
and the fridge-glass
becomes taller than me.

I look out of the window
and see buildings,
tall buildings.

Skyscrapers: you go to the nth floor,
and as you look down
you can get a high
from these tall high buildings,
looking up or down.

Mankind has always loved
tall, and taller buildings
everywhere.

Do they say something to you,
sprouting like mushrooms in the morning
dew?

Providing a high,
perhaps with similarity
to a tall-building high?

A high on tall buildings,
an architectural high
from those man-made, concrete buildings.

HIGHWAYS
(those necessary, unsung conveyors)

Found in a number of regions on this planet,
motorways that solemnly gleam
with entire continuity.

The Highway is a link,
a piece of communication
between places and ideas,
where you may see very fast vehicles
VRUUUOOOOOOooooom!

Highways link, connect, convey.
They feature a route
with a clear beginning and a clear end.

Bridges

Some highways feature viaducts, bridges;
such solid bridges
from one place to another.

People

Some people can be bridges,
for example, to a new idea.
Others can own metal, concrete bridges;
I have never met someone who is
and owns a bridge.

But I really do know
of highways that have bridges
and are also solid connections.

Landscapes

Some highways cross fields of wheat,
others trespass quiet deserts,
or swirl around the countryside,
embracing mountains.

Highways

A concrete feature of our days.

We wonder about tomorrow -
how will we use it?

Watch and appreciate these highways,
stare at them in awe,
understand them thoroughly we must;
they were built for clear purposes,
they have a beginning and an end .

It can be simple,
it could be abstruse,
it must be understood.

AIRPORTS

Scattered unevenly around the planet,
from these we can be taken
away.

Big, small,
built and designed by human hands,
places for good-byes, hellos,
kisses, and heavy hearts.

Few men or women go to an airport to fly;
most will never take off,
most will never soar,
mentally, spiritually,
always, *permanently*, grounded.

DUSK AT AIRPORTS

Softly dying sunlight reflected on metal.
Yeah, soon they'll be flying,
the machines above us.

Power from chemical reactions
propelling the equipment that now
solemnly encloses us, our aluminum shirt
that takes us away.

We shall land again,
at another airport.
We shall remember, if so,
what was left at each airport
the good-byes, kisses, heavy hearts.

Airports, from there
we can be taken away.

THE ACROBATIC ASTRONAUT
– PART III

Flung into the sky again after
a respite on Earth to kiss his wife
and pay the credit card bill,
our Acrobatic Astronaut is back
to the seemingly endless space station.

His is just an ordinary job.

With a powerful telescope
he spots a crowd there on Earth
who think their God really knows,
and they and only they possess
the true meaning of Life and Death
and such. But that other crowd
doesn't agree, so they go killing each other
to work out who will really *be*.

Our Astronaut spots a fireman saving
a small baby from a crumbling building.
The baby, not the fireman's kin,
will survive. Why?
No easy biologic logic there.

Spotting another crowd
at a football match – their eyes following
a sphere bloated with Uncertainty
shouting, whistling,
having fun with Uncertainty.

He resumes his job, an ordinary job,
pressing buttons and so on,
sometimes checking, his mind not fretting
over the issues and facts below
on this Earth that is still ours.

CITIES AND NON-CITIES

Last time we came back from the space station,
waving good-bye, see-you-soon
to our friend the Acrobatic Astronaut,
structures were spotted; some structures
that insist on dotting this planet.

These formations are called cities,
but other structures also endure
perhaps more crystalline and pure,
call them non-cities.

Non-cities consist of almost
(quite important this 'almost')
everything that cities don't feature.

Non-cities are, most of the time
free of city-like things
such as cars
such as new shoes
such as old ideas
maybe out of use.

Oceans, forests, deserts
and, strangely, highways,
become therefore non-cities,
so simple.

CONCRETE

Men built a city.
Seed fell in the city and grew
becoming a tree.

The tree grew, the city grew.

Now there is concrete
around the tree.
Sidewalks encircle it,
roots slowly but surely breaking
the concrete which yields
to the natural power of the tree.

Man against Nature?
I beg to disagree.

As concrete comes from Man,
Man comes from Nature;
concrete becomes therefore
Natural.

Think about it.

FLUID WATER

It's almost everywhere
if you pay attention
to its many aspects
in and on this planet –
it is the basis of Life.

Puddles, lakes, creeks
rivers and then
the sea,
oceans.

Smaller, the drizzle, rain,
your own faucet in
that convenient house of yours
may one day be dry.

Waterless.

Is it a drought?
(in the desert in your tent or home
water may be scarce)

But you, my friend,
my urban friend,
you will tend
to take it for granted.

As if water
will be permanently available.

Inside your body?
Water.

No water
no life.

Thoroughly understand.
Don't take it for granted.
What is really happening?

UNEXPECTED ADDITION OF BLACK CLOUDS

There was a flower floating on the river,
moving with the river's flow,
at times fast, at times slow.

Some rivers are devoid of fish
but not of rotten filth;
some men have spoiled rivers
and some rivers, filthy or not,
may feature floating flowers.

Some rivers can get angry
and, by calling brother-rain
(both made of the same stuff),
flood, with consequences dire.

Some men are devoid of reason
but not of stupid behaviour,
and they have spoiled cities,
and they have spoiled lives.

There was a flower floating on the river.

WHALE IN THE SKY

It's a whale-shaped cloud;
you see the body, the tail,
you see the fins and the spray.
Movement is slow,
cloudly and whale-like slow
(there is little wind...)

But the form is there;
airborne mass,
some type of gas,
(mostly vapour, we know).

Sailors sometimes say
whales solemnly smile;
now this one has.

Now it is losing the shape
fading away, away;
disappeared yes, but the impression
hereby candidly registered.

GASEOUS CONVERSATION

Hello, I'm the Earth's atmosphere,
you've been breathing me these days
so I'm inside of you
and you're inside of me.

Hey, please see,
you've been producing so much pollution.
Just like me you are part
of nature, but think, think, think...

Your physics have split the Atom
but you've failed to understand me
I don't mind, mind, mind, mind...

Do not take me for granted
I may fail.
I'd like to think that you love me,
so don't sabotage the one you love.
Proceed nicely,
please proceed, proceed, proceed...

LOTS OF DEAD PEOPLE

Hurricane!
Lots of dead people.
My Lord...

Earthquake!
Lots of dead people.
Horrendous...

Floods!
Lots of dead people.
How terrible...

War!
Lots of dead people.
Avoidable.

PROBLEM SOLVING IN THE NEOLITHIC

We have been watching them,
those yellow-haired people,
they came from the cold vasts,
they know we are here.

We saw them hunting
in the woods gazelle and deer,
big mammoths in the fields;
our gazelle, our mammoth.

Winds have been changing,
winter may be closing in.
Wonder if our horde will have
food enough for another passage.

We'll need more game,
we will need more food.
Those strange new people –
we know that we should

solve our problem.
A quiet raid after dewfall.
We know where to head
and we'll kill them all.

COMPETITION,
COMPETITION,
COMPETITION

If life becomes a crazy race,
remember Judah Ben-Hur;
hold your horses, hold your horses,
loosen the mind-reins only at the exact moment
and then...

FEAR

Are you afraid of poets?
You should be;
your regular thoughts and ideas
may be shuffled and bent
in a way that's not clear.
So maybe, yes, consider having
a little bit of fear.

But to think
that poems change minds,
bend hearts, could be just
wishful thinking.

NEW SHOES

Some people have shoes,
others don't, don't, don't.
Some people have dreams,
others sleep a dreamless sleep.

Some guys buy new shoes
and I just got myself a pair
of brand new shoes.

New shoes make you want to,
make you want to walk;
we shall walk.

Makes me very optimistic
about those new strange places
Where will my new shoes take me?

You see, after all
I do have dreams,
conveyed by a simple pair
of new shoes.

OF PATHS AND LINES

Have you seen my old friend?
Do you know his whereabouts?
For some time now
I haven't heard from him.

It left me a little abashed.
We parted some years ago;
will I ever find my old friend?

Circumstances, and such and such,
made our paths differ,
and our ways diverge.
Divergent yesterday.

The lines of one's life
are not straight lines,
they tend to be curves,
never infinite.

We could then expect
to understand the possibility
of life-lines again crossing
and we'll meet again.

RENEWED PERSPECTIVES

Perusing photographs from long ago,
he understands that colloquial convention
concerning his life-line.

Facts, faces and events
from a time when the dream
of today's situation was only that –
a dream which was never fully dreamt.

It became another reality
of complicated quality.

This is the quest for intelligent integration
of past and present; it should only *be*.
Nothing poignantly philosophical here.

HER ADIABATIC SMILE

Memories of an almost-love, a Systems Analyst by profession

As I admire your true, very candid,
adiabatic smile, that fosters thoughts
about the systems you possess,

I wonder what's going on in your mind:
the ideas you process-think
within the logic in-between,
your blithe, controlled heart;

your conclusions, arrays and interfaces
which colour your character
(lovely as free daisies
floating on a virtual stream).

It is not passion,
it is a force;
it is not biological desire,
it is attraction –
electro-magnetic attraction,
precise, mathematically, just as you would
like it.

THE ANVIL

There remains the Anvil:
sturdy, silent, solemn,
always ready to work.

Anvil-men: not easy to find
but then, when called to action
they do deliver, those Anvil-Men,
they shape, taking the blow,
shaping new things.

They do not utter.
They reverberate.

SOME SUNSETS

Contemplate now and then
some really gorgeous sunsets
when the sky displays
marvellous colours of dusk
that here and there, glow,
fostering deep and unsettling ideas –
what do we really know?

It's crazy then, to realize
this atmosphere of ours
displays this solemn prize
delighting our silent eyes.

No ideas, no philosophy,
just plain effect of the light,
simultaneously infusing and fading.

Sunsets,
yeah, some sunsets.

PEE ON THE GRASS

I like to pee on the grass,
hearing the sound of it falling.

I like to pee on the grass;
I feel natural, entire,
part of Nature by just
candidly peeing on the grass.

I like to imagine that superstring
maybe bringing something unusual,

while I gently pee on the grass,
under an unyielding sky
watching the stars that observe us.

HUGE AND STRANGE

Eventually we will invent
strange things to do, to see,
things to make us happy.
This feeling is not only ours.
Let us eventually invent.

He is walking on the beach.
Suddenly, his hand reaches
for an unusual, forgotten shell.
He flings it away into the sea.

He did this because he knows
that the day, the sea, the tide,
shall bring the shell back
to be found again and flung
into the almost-same sea.

Everything that's strange is huge.
We're on this Earth to laugh.
We invent strange things
like throwing shells into the sea.

Just to have
a small laugh.

SPACE-TIME

Sometimes one may experience space-time.
If you really concentrate, it may be felt;
no more seconds, no more minutes.

You feel heavy, you feel light,
you feel whole, you think bright,
you get the structure, all and part,
think of Science, but need the *Art*.

Then a new pace.
The mind loses self, selfishness,
integrates with alacrity
into opalescence.

BIRDIES

It's a nice sunny morning
with singing birds galore.

Birds sing for biological reasons,
not to please some silly poet.

But then, they do.

SOME OBSERVATIONS AND NOTHING ELSE

'Scary Scarecrows' – yes, The Seventh Law of Thermodynamics is yet to be established.

'Cabral's Vulture' – to extract poetry from such an uncanny, ugly animal is really something, and that is what J.Cabral did in the 'O Urubu Mobilizado' ('The Mobilised Vulture').

'The Acrobatic Astronaut' – inspired by David Bowie's Major Tom.

'Time And Kalashnikovs' – the AK-47 became a well-known weapon that wounds, cripples and kills people.

'Schrödinger's Cat' – experience shows, at the same time, how our knowledge can be Magic and limited.

'Gaseous Conversation' – the Atmosphere is changing, fast.

'Problem Solving In The Neolithic' –
reminds us of what we were (and still are)
– intelligent, murderous apes. Will we
overcome this? When?

'Competition, Competition, Competition'
– refers to the classic Hollywood movie *Ben
Hur*, and overcoming horrendous situations.

'Fear' – what is the real sense or power of
poetry?

'Pee On The Grass' – the Superstring
Theory states that there are not only the
regular four dimensions (Time included)
but eleven ones. Although controversial,
the Maths is beautiful. The theory broadly
suggests that we do not know everything,
but we are aware that we do not know
everything.

ACKNOWLEDGEMENTS

Thanks to the editor Cate Myddleton-Evans, at Eyewear Publishing (Maida Vale), Todd Swift and Edwin Smet for his book design.

OTHER MAIDA VALE TITLES

Chris Moore – *Barbell Buddha*
Eric Sigler/Donald Langosy – *The Poet's Painter*
David Fox-Pitt – *Positiverosity*
Carol Susan Nathanson –*Last Performance At The Odeon*

Maida Vale is an imprint of Eyewear Publishing Ltd,
and is proud to work with authors to develop their rich and
complex literary projects, from memoirs to self-help, poetry to
novels. Our list is growing, and has so far included artists and
poets from Miami and Boston, a famous fitness guru,
and a Brazilian scientist-poet.